Copyright © 1995 by Arthur Pine
Cover design © 1995 by Sourcebooks, Inc.

All rights reserved. No part of this book may be reproduced in any form or by any electronic or mechanical means including information storage and retrieval systems—except in the case of brief quotations embodied in critical articles or reviews—without permission in writing from its publisher, Sourcebooks, Inc.

Published by: **Sourcebooks, Inc.**
P.O. Box 372, Naperville, Illinois, 60566
(708) 961-3900
FAX: (708) 961-2168

Editorial: Todd Stocke
Cover Design: Wayne Johnson
Interior Design: Wayne Johnson, Sourcebooks, Inc.
Production: Andrew Sardina

ISBN: 1-57071-070-8

Printed and bound in the United States of America.
10 9 8 7 6 5 4 3 2 1

Unexpected Roads

A Personal Success Journal

ARTHUR PINE
with Julie Houston

Naperville, IL

*U*nexpected roads are waiting to be traveled.

No matter what situation you are in, *you will land on your feet again* if you have complete confidence in yourself and your abilities.

> "The choice is between doing something and doing nothing, and doing nothing never gets you anywhere."
> *Felix G. Rohatyn,*
> *American financier*

Look ahead, think, and plan for what you want to accomplish, not just now, but in the years ahead.

Determine your assets and skills and how you can apply them in other areas.

Nothing is impossible.

I believe in me—
that's what you've got to
say to yourself.

*H*ope is the greatest remedy of all.

Many people dismiss their ability to "think creatively" when a door closes. That kind of defeatist attitude is all wrong. Find ways to get your thinking out of a rut and new ideas will come.

*L*ife is full of surprises.

*F*ate is what you make of it.

Sometimes a momentous change of plans unexpectedly alters circumstances, quickly turning disappointment into rare opportunity.

How you see yourself is important because it reflects on how others see you.

"If at first you don't succeed, try, try again. Then quit. There's no use being a damn fool about it."
W.C. Fields
(1879-1946)

Opportunities come along whether you're ready for them or not. They either happen, or you make them happen.

*I*f everything you do turns out to be right, then you are one of the few lucky geniuses in this world.

"To be defeated and yet not surrender, that is victory."
Jozef Pilsudski (1867-1935), Polish national hero and freedom fighter

Go in with an open mind and find out for yourself whether a new opportunity exists.

Yes, you can do anything you want to do.

If there is a chance in a million that you can do something, anything, to keep what you want from ending, it is worth a try.

With all its faults, on balance, it's still a wonderful world— if you have the right outlook on life.

If changing your situation seems too overwhelming a challenge, think of short-term goals at first.

Never take no for an answer.

It doesn't matter how many times you fail, all you need is one success.

Persistence pays off.

"It takes twenty years to make an overnight success."
Eddie Cantor (1892-1964), American comedian

Keep an upbeat attitude as you struggle through.

Don't take a silent response to be a negative response.

Hopelessness is a relative state.

Absolutism in anything is ridiculous… Embrace change, and great happiness is out there waiting for you.

"A man should learn to detect and watch that gleam of light which flashes across his mind from within, more than the luster of the firmament of bards and sages."
Ralph Waldo Emerson

You can't succeed
every time.

Use the feeling of defeat as your motivation to get out of a bad situation.

It may take several changes before landing solidly on your feet, but do not give up.

*E*verything has a purpose; everything has its own time.

> "Care, thought, and study go into making something succeed; luck is something you get playing the lottery, a roulette game, or gambling."
> Wess Roberts, *Author of Leadership Secrets of Attila the Hun*

Just because it may be raining in the morning, doesn't mean the sun won't shine before the day is over.

Turn a situation over and over in your mind until that new idea emerges.

*E*nvision your success in communicating your message, not your failure. Breathe freely, stand tall and keep your body relaxed.

Don't get hung up on appearance. If you feel good about yourself, you will make doors open.

*T*ake your time and think through your situation. Just wait and see— something great will come of it if you don't let it get you down.

*L*ook upon a setback as a temporary bump on the road to success and better times.

Try, stop, and think.
Then try again.

Good seldom comes by mistake.

One of the best ways to give yourself some distance from a bad situation is having a sense of humor, especially about yourself and your circumstances.

If you have trouble
accepting yourself
for who you are,
be open to getting
outside help.

"You can commit no greater folly than to sit by the roadside until someone comes along and invites you to ride with him to wealth or influence." *John B. Gough (1817-1886)*

Whatever your initial reaction, *you must take action* if you are ever going to move ahead. You can't let rejection get you down.

Closing a door on injustice, deceit, or harassment takes great courage and may even bring dire consequences, but the truth provides peace of mind.

There are no guarantees in life.

Don't just dream about the possibilities for making a new start. Plan your exit.

People are not born optimists or pessimists; it is the attitude they assume that forms their outlook. You are the one who makes that determination.

Your biggest break can come from never quitting.

Mobilize the support of others to help you win.

"By the streets of 'by and by' one arrives at the house of 'never.'"
Miguel de Cervantes (1547-1616)

Cultivate a genuine interest in people.

Look for ways to help others when they need it, and go out of your way to help them.

*F*ind that "extra something" in your background and experience that will give you an edge on the competition.

Show yourself to be a generous, upbeat person at all times, understanding of other people's problems and ready to lend a hand.

Your manner and attitude count just as strongly as your ability to give a good performance.

A door could open when you need it the most.

Show your appreciation for favors, large and small.

> "If opportunity doesn't knock... build a door."
> *Milton Berle,*
> *Comic/Entertainer*

It is very satisfying to know you have helped someone—give that satisfaction in return for assistance.

Never end a relationship on a sour note or with an argument.

*T*ake time out—
to think!

You don't have to be a genius to think creatively about making new doors open; all it takes is ingenuity and common sense.

Bad news? Share it! You'd be surprised at how people can help you if you just let them know your situation.

Am I ever going to show them they made a mistake! That's the attitude to take when a door closes on you. Let it fire you up to work harder, to move ahead faster.

"Temperate anger well becomes the wise." *Philemon (370-260 BC), Athenian comic poet*

Don't do it in a self-serving way, but use your self-respect as a source of courage to speak out if you must close a door.

*D*on't let a negative attitude be an obstacle.

When a door closes, use constructive anger as a positive force to open new doors.

"Great dreams are often so far away from your reach that you can become discouraged. But each small goal you achieve gives you confidence to try the next."
*John H. Johnson,
Publisher,
Ebony magazine*

*I*t's never too late to move ahead.

Don't think the light you see coming in the tunnel is only an oncoming train— it may be an angel in disguise.

*L*isten to others,
but make up your
own mind.

"Victories that are easy are cheap. Those only are worth having which come as the result of hard fighting."
Henry Ward Beecher (1813-1887), American clergyman

Be willing to let things go. When you find yourself at an impasse or about to get into an argument, stop and think before you blow off steam.

Keep up your courage when it comes to dealing with difficult people. You may be tested severely—at the very same time that you are given the chance to accomplish your goals.

Don't be intimidated by reputation...find ways to win people over to your side.

Don't let ego
stand in your way.

Keep up your contacts; reach out to others. It's all right to ask for help. People are more willing to help than you might think.

There's nothing wrong with a little ignorance.

> "The secret of success in life is for a man to be ready for his opportunity when it comes."
> *Benjamin Disraeli (1804-1881), English statesman and author*

Keep your eyes open for serendipity. The perfect door may be in front of you, but you must be prepared to recognize it.

Broadcast, don't hide, your age and experience.

The darkest moments
can turn out to
the good.

Don't let the right
time pass you by.

Be patient with the steps it takes, emotionally and physically, to make a new door open.

Put yourself
in the vicinity
of your dreams.

If you can get yourself to believe that it's a wonderful world, it will probably turn out that way for you.

Analyze the source of your unhappiness before you plan your next move.

*P*roceed slowly,
but do proceed.

It is much simpler to open a door with a smile than with a frown.

*D*on't be afraid to have a change of heart—before it may be too late.

Increase your chances of meeting new people, of being at the right place at the right time.

Stick to your dreams. Do everything you can to realize them. The rest will take care of itself.

Expand your interests. Consider volunteer work for the local hospital, park, or school.

Join or establish a group that attracts like-minded people. Whatever your "community of interest," put yourself where you will meet other people.

Keep your head
and don't panic
when a door
appears to close.

What have you got to lose?

"What is defeat? Nothing but education; nothing but the first step to something better."
Wendell Phillips (1811-1884), American orator and reformer

Work, work, work—
but always with a
winning attitude.

*D*on't let difficult people hold you back from opportunity.

"Find a need and fill it—but don't resort to gimmicks! If you fill a real need, you'll have a loyal following."
*Adrien Arpel,
Founder of her own multimillion-dollar cosmetics company*

Pursue your areas of interest. Activities that give you special pleasure are a powerful resource in helping you meet new people who share those interests.

Give yourself a second chance.

Look your situation over carefully; put certainty into perspective.

"Great opportunities come to all, but many do not know they have met them."
Albert Elijah Dunning (1844-1923), American editor

*L*ook for ways to harness your talents in new areas.

There isn't any mountain you can't climb once you get off to the right start.

A reversal isn't always the end of the road, it may just be a detour.

Network. One contact leads to another—in a sense, that's what life is all about. Be willing to ask for favors, at the same time be willing to perform them.

You may not feel upbeat, but try acting it anyway. You will be surprised at how quickly your bad mood is dispelled.

*D*etermine your priorities.

When a door closes, have the confidence to think big—to stand up and say, "This is what I want to do." Go after it.

Many doors may close before the right one opens.

Your original hopes and aspirations for a career may suddenly end, but who knows, that devastating closed door may lead you to another that opens onto an exciting new path in life.

Believe in your abilities.
Try something new and
different and you will
make it.

Challenge conventional wisdom when looking for a job.

Associate with upbeat people.

Conventional wisdom can be challenged to make way for new opportunities. Look, listen and debunk. Don't let "standard procedures" defeat you.

Never give up on the ones you love.

> "Truth is not only violated by falsehood; it may be equally outraged by silence."
> *Henri Frederic Amiel (1821-1881), Swiss philosopher*

"Stars may be seen from the bottom of a deep well, when they cannot be discerned from the top of a mountain." *Charles Haddon Spurgeon (1834-1892), English clergyman*

Accept the prospect
of change.

*L*ook for ways you can reciprocate favors.

"We are always in the forge or on the anvil; by trials, God is shaping us for higher things."
Henry Ward Beecher (1813-1887), American clergyman

Let others hear from you in their time of suffering.

It's just as easy to be happy as it is to be miserable—so the choice is yours.

If you spot a glimmer of hope behind a door that you hate to see close, take immediate action.

Don't let negative emotions get the better of you. If you are miserable, make new plans and act on them.

You must put up a fight to make miracles happen.

Take the initiative to make changes for the better. It may not happen all at once, but keep up your efforts.

Put yourself first.
As difficult as it may be,
do not be afraid to close
a door on someone.

*E*ven in the gravest situations, hope exists if we choose to find it.

"Tears hinder sorrow from becoming despair."
J.H. Leigh Hunt (1784-1859), English author

Make up your mind what is important to you; what comes first and how to find a balance between job, family, your outside interests, or whatever it may be.

Caring can start a domino effect.

Hold back on making judgments. Go in with an open mind and find out for yourself whether a new opportunity exists.

*T*ough times become like gym equipment. Just ask anyone who has weathered the worst: it makes you tougher.

*T*ake control of today,
let tomorrow take
care of itself.

Do not deny the expression of anger or grief—or any emotion for that matter.

Consider every inch that allows light into a dark situation a triumph.

> Taking a more satisfying job at a lower level may very well be a terrific move for you if it gives you the time you have always wanted to spend with your family, or pursuing a hobby, or traveling.

Try anything. Chances are you will have a lot of fun in the process of opening doors, and eventually luck will come your way.

Ingenuity can provide you with a golden opportunity to move ahead.

A steady, friendly rapport will ultimately serve you well.

"An enterprise, when fairly once begun, Should not be left till all that ought is won."
William Shakespeare
(1564-1616)

Think of changing your role in the game if it keeps you in what you love.

The same punch that knocks the passive fighter flat causes the fighter who is determined to win to fall back momentarily before regaining his balance.

Changes—doors closing, doors opening—actually occur all through life despite anything we do about them.

*U*se the closed door as your inspiration to accomplish more than you ever thought you could.

Fantastic New Journals From Sourcebooks!

Random Acts: A Kindness Journal
Guided by the quotes, suggestions and tips from the original bestselling *Random Acts of Kindness*, create a memoir of the little kindnesses you do for others and the everyday, wonderful things others do for you.

160 pages, ISBN: 1-57071-034-1 (paperback) $7.95

Awakening: A Personal Transformation Journal
For nearly 20 years, readers have been seeking a way to interact and connect with bestselling author Wayne Dyer. Featuring quotes, advice and suggestions from all of his books, *Awakening* is the perfect space for reflections on your journey to greater self-awareness.

160 pages, ISBN: 1-57071-071-6 (paperback) $7.95

Loving: A Journal Of Our Relationship
The new, interactive companion to Greg Godek's phenomenal bestseller *1001 Ways to Be Romantic*, this journal will help you inject romance into every day and every aspect of your relationship. Create your own personal romantic memoir!

160 pages, ISBN: 1-57071-058-9 (paperback) $7.95

Breathing Space: A Journal For Women Who Do Too Much
Let this elegant journal be the place where you find the peaceful time you deserve. Filled with quotes, inspirational suggestions, and tips from the bestselling book *Finding Time,* by Paula Peisner Coxe, *Breathing Space* reminds you that time to yourself is important.

160 pages, ISBN: 1-57071-036-8 (paperback) $7.95

Angel Thoughts: A Journal Of Faith And Reflection
Angel Thoughts is a terrific personal memoir and a perfect gift for those you love. This powerful journal will help you make faith and reflection an even greater part of your life. Filled with enlightening and inspiring quotes, it will hold your messages of hope.

160 pages, ISBN: 1-57071-059-7 (paperback) $7.95

To order these books or any other of our many publications, *please contact your local bookseller or gift store*, or call Sourcebooks at (708) 961-3900.

To receive a catalog of Sourcebooks' publications, please write to us at:
P.O. Box 372
Naperville, IL 60566